...et ...July ...e ...space of half-an-hour or so, in broad daylight, right next to one of the most visited sites in the world – Stonehenge. Measuring 900 by 500 feet, with 151 circles, the glyph was visited by thousands of people. The farmer wisely chose to charge an admission into the field, and recouped the cost of his damaged field many times over. This intricate glyph was one of two Julia Sets to appear in the summer of 1996, and was linked to fractals, and possibly chaos theory (or even the new vogue of chaos magic). Stonehenge is one of a number of places that attract crop circles over and over again through the years, along with Silbury Hill, the Punch Bowl at Cheesefoot Head and East Field at Alton Barnes, to name a few. However, Stonehenge appears to be one of the pivotal points in the world of crop circles, with a majority of the formations occurring within a forty-mile radius of the World Heritage site.

Natural conditions connected with crop circles

The Wessex Triangle

Crop circles are not a new phenomenon. Some farmers claim to have seen crop circles in their fields all their lives, as have their parents, and grandparents. They weren't reported because they didn't think there was anything unusual about them. In fact the circles may have been part of the landscape since pre-Celtic times. However, in the old days, country folk thought these enigmatic formations were the result of natural causes, with rutting deer or hedgehogs being the most likely suspects. Birds such as crows and rooks are also a common sight in fields of mature cereal crops, where they gather in a circle to feed on the ripened seed heads, trampling the crop underneath in a ring.

Other causes of circular damage were thought to be strange diseases, which the owner would certainly not want to talk about for fear of losing a buyer. Before the 1900s, circle damage was often attributed to fairies, or even the devil. In any case, the circles were often not reported, for economic reasons, fear of ostracism from the community and also because they weren't thought of as unusual.

With few exceptions, crop circles are created at night. Although they may appear most of the year, conditions are only right for viewing them between early April and late September in Wessex. All other attempts to pin them down are fruitless. They may or may not depend on local weather conditions, although they do appear rain, shine or fog. Close proximity to hills is not always necessary to their formation, as some have suggested. They have been found on all types of soil worldwide but the vast majority of English formations appear on 'aquiferous' rock strata which carry a lot of water, such as the chalk of Wessex. The force that often accompanies them can have a buzzing electronic sound, or a loud roar – or it can be completely silent. It might come from the sky, emanate from the earth, or both. Or neither.

A large proportion of the crop circles appear in the 'Wessex Triangle': its cardinal points are the areas around Silbury Hill, Warminster/Westbury and Winchester. Besides crop circles, the Triangle also boasts a large number of UFO reports, as well as the largest and oldest stone circles – Avebury and Stonehenge. It is

The Mowing - Devil :

Or, Strange NEWS out of

Hartford - shire.

Being a True Relation of a Farmer, who Bargaining with a Poor Mower, about the Cutting down Three Half Acres of Oats; upon the Mower's asking too much, the Farmer swore, That the Devil should Mow it, rather than He. And so it fell out, that that very Night, the Crop of Oat shew'd as if it had been all of a Flame; but next Morning appear'd so neatly Mow'd by the Devil, or some Infernal Spirit, that no Mortal Man was able to do the like.

Also, How the said Oats ly now in the Field, and the Owner has not Power to fetch them away.

Licensed, August 22th. 1678.

Left:

This Strange *NEWS from a seventeenth-century pamphlet must surely contain one of the earliest accounts of a crop circle and goes on to give a very serious reason for their existence:*

Men may dally with Heaven, and criticize on Hell, as Wittily as they please, but that there are really such places, the wise Dispensations of Almighty Providence does not cease continually to evince. For if by those accumulated circumstances which generally induce us to the belief of anything beyond our senses, we may reasonably gather that there are certainly such things as DEVILS, we must necessarily conclude that these Devils have a Hell: and as there is a Hell, there must be a Heaven, and consequently a GOD: and so all the Duties of Christian Religion as indispensable subsequents necessarily follow.

littered with burial mounds, many also circular. Silbury Hill is the largest man-made earthwork in Neolithic Europe. Considering the grandeur and sheer number of these ancient circular constructions, the question has to be asked: did the Neolithic farmers see crop circles being formed 5000 years ago, and build the temples to reflect the power that they held in awe? Many of the large single circles are close in size to Stonehenge.

Crop circles of the last twenty-five years

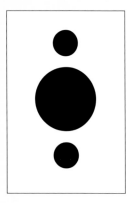

Above:

The first crop circle to gain national attention appeared at Cheesefoot Head, Hampshire 1981. Complexity of design has certainly increased since then.

Opposite:

Crop circles are frequently seen near ancient monuments. Here the hill carving of a white horse is seen towering over a formation in Cherhill, Wiltshire, in 1992 (inset) and at Hackpen Hill in 1999 (background).

The first crop circles to attract the attention of the media were the three circles found in The Punch Bowl, Cheesefoot Head, Hampshire, during late July, 1981. The centre circle measured 17 metres across, with the smaller ones measuring 8 metres each. Researchers had been studying singletons as early as the late 1970s, but with little interest from the press. Even after the Cheesefoot Head circles were found, there were still few reports up until the mid-1980s. These early circles were still mainly singletons, although it didn't take long for doubles, triples and quintuplets to show up in fairly rapid succession. In 1988, a little over 100 circles were reported. In 1989 300 were seen. This annual average has remained steady since.

The lack of physical evidence has always been frustrating for researchers studying the Loch Ness monster, Bigfoot and UFOs. Quite the opposite occurs when investigating crop circles. The evidence is there, in stunning and beautiful form, for all to see.

Crop circles are known for their crisp, sharp edges, unusual design and flattened plants. Often an agrigylph will be found in the middle of a field, with no visible trails leading into it. They are almost always within the selected field, although field boundaries have been crossed on notable occasions.

Entering a circle – for even the most intricate new glyphs retain some circular features – is like opening a wonderful present. The circle wall will be clearly demarked from the rest of the crop, with little overspray of flattened stems into the surrounding area. The plant stems will be flattened very hard to the ground, which is itself often almost cement-like. Although the plants in the circle are now lying horizontal, they will still be growing without any apparent harm. Sometimes a swirled centre, rising like a little tepee, can also be seen. Often, it is hard to see what form the glyph has taken, since they are best viewed from the air. All that can be seen are circles and lines of various sizes running off in every direction.

People entering crop circles experience a variety of physical and mental effects. Depending on the formation and on the individual, these can range from feelings of elation, psychic ability and peacefulness to nausea, disorientation and panic. A number of causes have been put forward to account for these effects, including earth magnetism, energy lines, pesticides and orgone energy amplified by a radioactive field. So, a word of warning (especially if you neglect to ask the farmer's permission before entering the field): Enter at your own risk!

Above:

This formation, Ring and Circles, *appeared 1 June 1998 in oats, a mile south-east of Avebury. The large ring was about 150ft in diameter. There were many magically bent stalks.*

Below:

Summer 1983 Cheesefoot Head, Hants. A simple design.

Obviously, the designs have to be perfectly formed, with sharp edges and no overspill into the surrounding crop. The surest sign of a hoax is poor construction, dirt on the plants, and holes in the ground where poles could have been used as pivots. A true circle just feels right, which is rather hard to explain and only comes with practice. That's not exactly scientific, but neither is dowsing, but that's being used more and more recently. A true crop circle will dowse true, and will emit certain kinds of energy in distinct patterns. Most faked pictograms produce no results at all according to most dowsers. This might show that the act of making circles, at least in certain specific areas, can actually change the energy patterns in the locale. The pattern of a hoaxed site will be different, though.

The most important thing to look at is the way the plants are bent. In true formations, all the plants are bent to the ground, and yet none of broken or dead. This is especially hard to accomplish in rapeseed, which has the consistency of celery.

How are they bent? One theory is that the crop circles are somehow microwaved. For instance, when the stem of a plant is cut, a malty smell can be detected, which might suggest that they have been cooked from the inside. Also, in some cases, the ground water in the area around crop circles has vanished, with the resulting soil dry and parched, even if it has been raining. Exhaustive lab analysis into hundreds of crop circles from 1991–99 by biophysicist Dr W.C. Levengood reveals changes that have taken place inside affected plants. Often the nodes have been blown open (expulsion cavities), which would take a rapid rate of heating to accomplish. The seed cavities are often elongated and abnormal developments in the germination rate of the seeds were often noted.

When you take into account all of the above, it does seem possible that the plants have been exposed to short, intense bursts of microwave radiation. Some people have displayed symptoms of negative effect from the energy source after spending too much time in formations.

The earliest hoaxers (at least the best known) were a pair of elderly gentlemen named Doug and Dave, both artists. They achieved a certain amount of fame (or notoriety) when they claimed to have proof, that they created the first set of glyphs which were clearly different from the original circles, stating that the whole thing started as a joke which had got out of hand. The crops were allegedly flattened using a plank held with a piece of rope, and later with a garden roller.

Beginning in 1991, the so-called insectogram designs were hailed by many as a profound example of alien intelligence or cosmic conciousness, and definitely genuine. Doug and Dave said that the presence of two loop-like features in many of these insect-like shapes were in fact their initials, DD, and that this proved their involvement, but many disputed this.

Obviously, these two men could not have created many of the agriglyphs. Many of the people who make crop circles say that they feel they are creating sacred art. In fact, while they are creating the formations, they feel they are being watched and protected by a higher intelligence. They also develop a strong spiritual sense that stays with them afterwards. Even Doug (of Doug and Dave fame) has claimed that they were being used by a higher power while they were making the crop circles. Sometimes the attraction of crop circles become too great, and there are cases of serious researches who have 'gone to the other side' and become hoaxers themselves (all in the name of research, they claim!).

Many elements of sacred geometry seem to play a part in many of the circles. For instance, multiples of sacred numbers 3 and 7 occur throughout the measurements. These same numbers have been used through the centuries by the relatively recent builders of great cathedrals new and old – perhaps all the way back to Stonehenge.

Above:
From a pencil sketch by John Newman, this crop circle, Plea for Peace, is a combination of the Hebrew Star of Solomon with the Islamic crescent moon – the symbols of the two faiths which have been at war for over a thousand years in the Middle East – and was tragically cut down by the farmer within 24 hours.

The 100+ft formation appeared on 5 August 1998 in Bishops Cannings.

Left:
This close-up shows the distinctive swirled pattern of the floor of a crop circle. Notice the sharp edge between the floor and the wall of the formation.

The Modern Development of Crop Circles

ooking back over the last fifteen years or so, it is interesting to see how the crop circles have changed and evolved. In the early to mid-1980s, the crop circles were just that – circles, with or without other smaller circles, in the crops. Towards the middle to the late 1980s, the circles began to form outside rings, and, with the smaller circles, formed patterns, such as the Celtic cross.

The years from 1990 saw a significant development in crop circles. A big change was to occur in the way we would view the circles, for now they were unmistakable designs, in the form of outerspace-type insects that incorporated circles, arcs and straight lines. Other designs that appeared included a number of fish or porpoises, then representations of astronomical events. The Asteroid Belt (see page 13) and the Earth Missing formations are examples of these. These agriglyphs were unquestionably made by some type of intelligence – whether human or non-human has yet to be conclusively proven.

In 1991, the glyphs became obvious symbols. On 17 July 1991, one of the most spectacular pictograms ever seen appeared in a field of wheat below the ancient hillfort of Barbury Castle near Swindon, supposed by some to be the site of King Arthur's greatest victory (Mount Badon).

The Mandlebrot, an important crop formation, was found on 12 August 1991, in the village of Ickleton, near Cambridge, curiously close to a certain hallowed hall of learning. A Mandlebrot Set is perhaps the most complex mathematical object, creating infinite dimensions.

As the Mandlebrot Set is involved with chaos theory, could the makers of this formation be asking us to consider the fine line between chaos and order, the 'just about right' spot we as humans, inhabit? Perhaps it is a warning that if we continue our destructive ways, we could cross the line into chaos again.

Above:
12 August 1991, Ickfield, Cambridgeshire, The Ickfield Mandlebrot. *Dr Gerald Hawkins discovered that deviations from proper M-set geometry in the formation allowed it to conform to the diatonic (musical) ratios found in earlier formations.*

The Ickfield Mandlebrot

glyph was situated in a place of power, and certain events that occurred close to the time of its creation, like a loud roaring noise and strange lights in the sky, lent it an air of majesty.

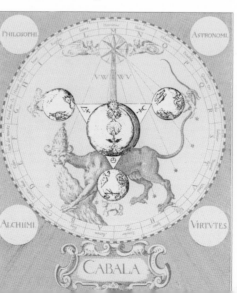

Left:
The engraving from the book Cabala, Speculum Altis et Naturae in Alchymia *published in 1654, bears an uncanny resemblance to the Barbury glyph.*

Circle Types

Above:

This stunning 295ft fractal arrived on 9 July 1998, in the East Field at Alton Barnes surrounded by 147 little circles and with a thick, tightly twisted 'bird's nest' of wheat in the centre.
The grey lines indicate where the crop was laid in different directions.

Below:

The Nine *arrived July – August 1998, Danebury Ring hill fort, Hampshire.*
The Nine.

Circles of all types are still found, along with the usual bugs, dolphins and arcane symbols. A brief look at the patterns through the years shows an unmistakable cycle. The shapes begin as simple circles, then multiply to doubles, triples and more. Next, rings start to surround the circles. Around 1990, space bugs begin to appear on the land, as well as lengthy hieroglyphics. Since then, each year has brought a new design element into the picture, while the circles, in their many variations, continue. The apparent themes in more recent years include planets and the solar system (a possible warning of things to come, such as the Hale-Bopp comet?) and mathematical models, from the Mandlebrot to the 1996 triple Julia Set on Windmill Hill, one of the most impressive formations yet seen.

The glory days of crop circles were certainly in the mid to late 1990s, leading up to some spectacular formations. However, the magic had worn off a bit by then, due in large part to hoaxers and disinformation campaigns, as well as bickering amongst the faithful. The formations up to the year 2000 developed themes set by earlier glyphs, while also producing completely new designs. Those that didn't owe anything to precursors often tried to feature an element of three-dimensionality, as in the cube-shaped crop circle. Different methods of forming the lays of the circles were also used. As in the past, many of the same locations were used over and over – East Field, the areas near Silbury and Avebury, the A4 between Marlborough and Calne. Most of these areas have two things in common; they have a special spiritual significance, and they are on the New Age tourist route, making any design easily seen by an appreciative audience.

In the summer fields we still see spirals, fractals, obvious symbols from esoteric traditions, along with triangles, squares and everything in-between. The rapid rate of evolution of the designs seems to have levelled off. Perhaps there is only so much that can be done in crops, or perhaps the evolution has turned inward, to

Left:
The Queen, *a remarkable 400ft formation arrived 6 August 1998, near Lockeridge, Wiltshire.*

affect the viewer unconsciously. Hopefully, if they continue, there will be designs we haven't even dreamt about yet in the fields of the new millennium.

Left:
The Beckhampton Mandala *arrived 20 June 1998 at Avebury Trusloe, west of Beckhampton, Wiltshire.*

Above:
About 150ft from corner, Fractal Fantasy *appeared 17 August 1998 north of Avebury, below Hackpen Hill, Wiltshire.*

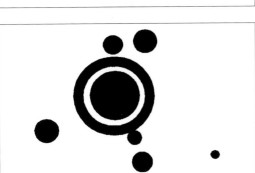

Left:
14 June 1991, Avebury, Wiltshire.

Left:
1 June 1996, Devizes. First formation sighted in Wiltshire that year.

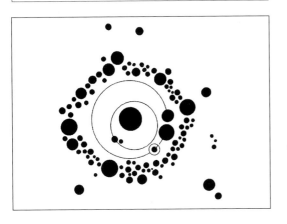

Left:
The Asteroid Belt, *June 1995 at Bishop's Sutton, Hampshire.*

Above:
The Diatom, *appeared 7 July 1998, Farnham, Hampshire.*

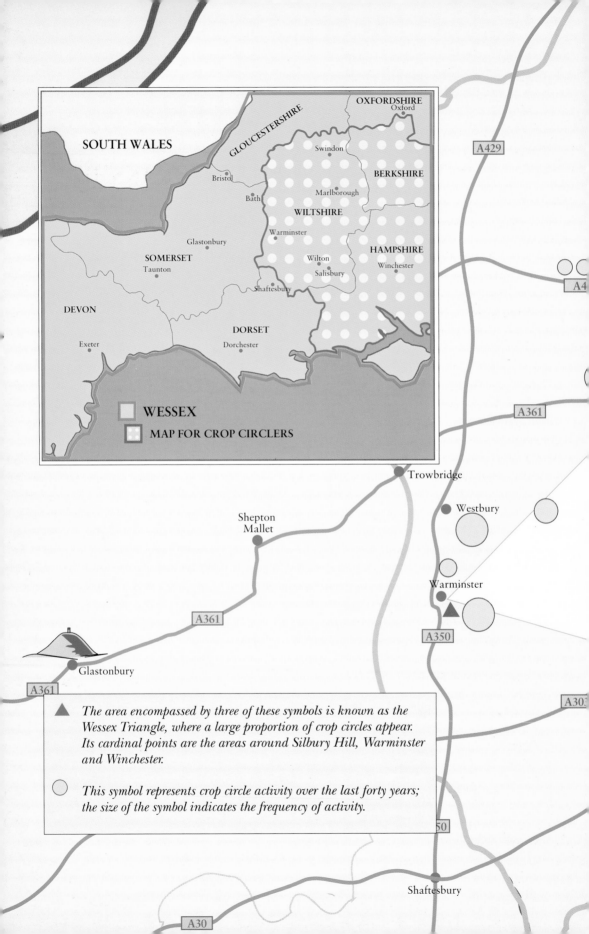

SOUTH WALES

GLOUCESTERSHIRE

OXFORDSHIRE
Oxford

Swindon

Bristol

BERKSHIRE

Bath

Marlborough

WILTSHIRE

Warminster

Glastonbury

HAMPSHIRE

SOMERSET

Wilton

Winchester

Taunton

Salisbury

Shaftesbury

DEVON

DORSET

Exeter

Dorchester

☐ **WESSEX**
▦ **MAP FOR CROP CIRCLERS**

A429

A4

A361

A361

Trowbridge

Shepton
Mallet

Westbury

A361

Warminster

A350

A303

Glastonbury

A361

▲ *The area encompassed by three of these symbols is known as the Wessex Triangle, where a large proportion of crop circles appear. Its cardinal points are the areas around Silbury Hill, Warminster and Winchester.*

◯ *This symbol represents crop circle activity over the last forty years; the size of the symbol indicates the frequency of activity.*

50

A30

Shaftesbury

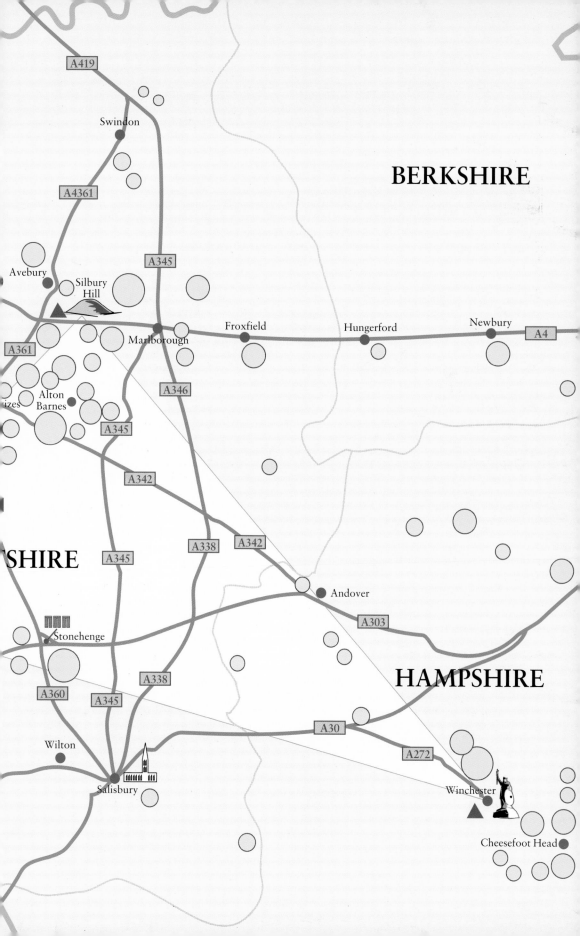

Eye Witnesses

Above:

It was reported that local people observed a green glow in the area shortly before the arrival of this pictogram and others later saw a rosy light over the formation, which appeared 27 June 1998 near Ostrava, the Czech Republic.

Of course, no one has ever seen a circle being formed. Or have they? Contrary to popular belief, there are a number of reports from witnesses to the event. One well-known account tells of how the witness heard the crop around emit a hissing sound while the seedheads shook violently. Then, within a few seconds, all the plants fanned out into a circular shape on the ground. The entire process took less than a minute. This occurred on a summer day without any clouds or wind. Other reports tell of a large, semi-transparent floating ball of light, usually orange or white, that was seen to pass slowly along a field, bounce once on the ground, and float away. The next day, a crop circle would appear where the ball touched the ground.

Other examples of bright lights abound. Many times they appear solid and gleaming and have been filmed on occasion. These solid lights are usually small, about the size of a large beach ball, and are seen skimming over the seed heads. Sometimes the UFO has appeared as a coloured column of light shooting electric charges of some kind to the ground, where a pictogram would later appear. Balls of light are quite common around crop circles. I have witnessed one myself, hovering over Golden Ball Hill in Wiltshire during the day. My great excitement was soon abated when local researchers casually informed me that 'they're only amber gamblers. We see 'em all the time around here.'

In addition to lights, unusual sounds also go hand-in-hand with new crop circles. One in particular, a strange trilling noise that has been captured on tape, is the most common. Sceptics assume this sound is nothing more than a bird, but in fact, when circles are formed there is an eerie absence of all the usual background noise caused by insects and birds.

Circles often have physiological effects on the visitor ranging from feelings of elation, joy and clarity to sensations of nausea, fatigue, metallic tastes in the mouth and disorientation. In certain instances, people claim to have been healed of physical complaints and injuries, at least temporarily. It seems to be a case of being in the right place at the right time and in the right frame of mind. Some people can enter a formation and feel elation, while others can enter the same site and suffer loss of memory, dizziness or a host of other problems. These maladies could be caused by the powerful energies of the formations, or perhaps microwave radiation. Also, the farmers spray these fields with dangerous pesticides, not expecting the fields to be frequented by large groups of people. The type of effect experienced depends on the field, the ley, the design and maybe your own state of mind, since circles are known to act on a subconscious level with us.

The circles seem to have a telepathic effect, too. In some cases, researchers have hoped, privately, to see a certain type of design, only to find it the next day. And in the case of the aerial phenomenon, the viewer is drawn to look at the UFO, even when it has appeared silently and outside the normal field of vision.

Crop circles create an energy pattern that can also affect mechanical objects. Many times news crews have been frustrated when their cameras and other equipment failed to work. Animals, too, can feel the energy and take pains to avoid circles.

In many eye-witness accounts, unidentified flying objects have been seen either before, during or after a crop circle has been formed. These UFOs can appear in many shapes, including small lights, cylinders, large balls and even Ferris wheels. Sounds, such as crackling, hissing, trilling or electronic noise may or may not accompany sightings. Often the UFOs have been seen to touch the ground softly, rise and float away, to reveal a crop circle the next day. Others have seen glowing balls or coloured cylinders emit an arced beam from their position in the sky to the ground, near to where crop circles have later been found.

Certainly, UFOs have favoured the Wessex Triangle in the recent past. A major UFO flap occurred around the Warminster area during the 1970s, attracting international attention. As a matter of fact, the town has recently named itself UFO Capital of Europe! Curiously, the phenomenon died down in the late 1970s and crop circles began appearing in the surrounding fields a few years later. The eminent psychologist Carl Jung (a contemporary of Sigmund Freud) wrote that these anomalous lights in the sky were harbingers of great changes in the collective psyche, due to occur with the passing of the Age of Pisces into the Age of Aquarius. For many years, Earth has been under the sign of Pisces, with its emphasis on worry, and a tendency to avoid conflict and effort. Now we are entering Aquarius with its characteristics of compassion and love of beauty. He further explained that the UFOs were actively involved in bringing about the changes. If this is true, and they are responsible for making crop formations, the UFOs are probably using a previously unknown weather condition along with electromagnetic or microwave energy to scribe the pictograms. Perhaps the increasing intricacy of the glyphs are an attempt by unidentified foreign life-forms at communication with us.

Above:
Aquarius – independent,
original and creative.

Above:
Pisces – intuitive, but
vague and prone to worry.

The Windmill Hill Triple Julia Set

This pictogram, one of the last of 1996, was unanimously felt to be the absolute pinnacle of the crop circle pantheon. First reported on 29 July on Windmill Hill, near Yatesbury in Wiltshire. In keeping with the glyph's apparent love of ancient sites, this area is known to have been one of the first to be inhabited by the remote ancestors of today's Britons. The Windmill Hill culture was in place before the Celts and their priests, the Druids, ever set foot on these shores. Is it just a coincidence that the most modern and impressive formation was found on the oldest site?

This formation, a three-armed spiral of 194 circles, was truly awe-inspiring. It almost appears to have been frozen in mid-turn.

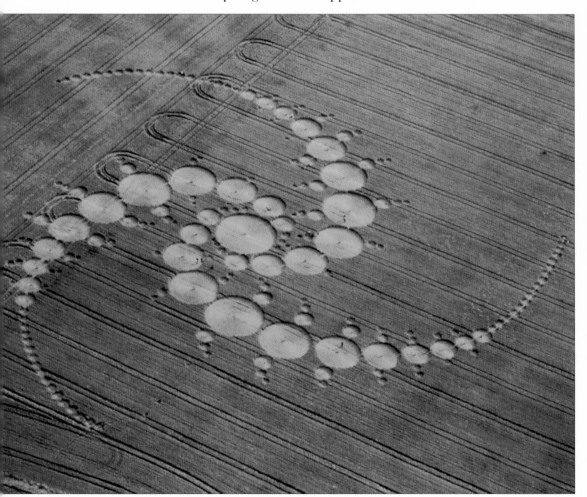

This design, at about 1000 feet, was also one of the largest ever recorded, and is obviously a progression of the fractal-based Stonehenge Julia set. In keeping with its grand design, the centres of the circles utilize every type of centre yet encountered – nests, fans, standing crop, and so on.

Biological causes have also been suggested as the cause of crop circles. Many point to the well-known fairy rings as examples. However, there are no known fungi that can create the intricate patterns seen in recent pictograms. Lightning strikes and whirlwinds are other contenders, but both cause great destruction, hardly the case in pictograms with their well-defined edges.

Biological causes of crop circles

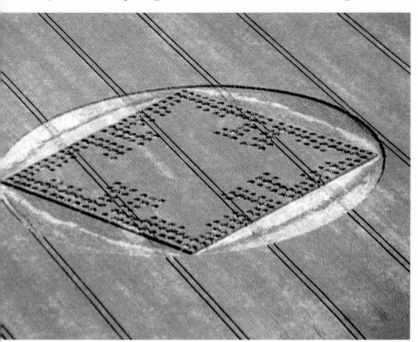

Left:
In 1999 Windmill Hill was again the site of an exceptional image. This one contained 288 small circles inside what was seen by some as the cross of the Knights Templar who once inhabited this landscape. Others saw here 'the floor plan of a mighty fortress or hallowed temple'.

The crop circles (or their makers) have been shown to be responsive to thought patterns. Certain researchers, who have wished (silently) to see a particular type of formation, have had it appear the next time they were looking. Organised meditations have also produced formations. The circles can link into our subconscious impulses and thoughts. Indeed, those who study crop circles run the same risk as paranormal researchers do – that whatever is controlling them is also able to enter the subconscious mind of the researcher, changing his or her view of the world, of reality itself.

The Subconscious

UFOs

Cymatics

Some crop circle researchers have been profoundly affected by the circles, even to the point of madness. In addition, the incredible power associated with UFOs sometimes dogs the researcher, causing a number of strange events to occur in his or her presence.

Are the crop circles trying to tell us something? Could they be a kind of communication – between galaxies, between the future and us? If we look at crop circles, we can see that they have evolved in complexity from year to year. Isn't that the same way as we teach language, by starting slowly and simply and gradually becoming more complex? However, no one has come forward (yet) claiming to have completely deciphered the code.

Suppose then that this is a language that isn't meant to be written. Perhaps it is a language that we understand within our bodies, our very DNA. The language of crop circles could be written in vibrations.

Cymatics is the name for the effects of vibrations on physical media such as water, oil and sand. It was developed in 1967 by Swiss scientist Hans Jenny. By transmitting sound of various frequencies through a medium, he was able to capture the exact geometric pattern of each frequency. Interestingly, as the complexity of the frequencies rose, so too did the complexities of the cymatic shapes.

And so we must ask ourselves: are crop circles the cymatic patterns left on the ground because there has been a rise in the vibrations of the earth?

Strange lights in the sky have been known in England for centuries.
On 8 December 1733, a certain Mr Cracker of Fleet, Dorset saw *Something in the sky
which appeared in the north, but vanished from my sight, as it was intercepted by trees …
On a sudden it re-appeared, darting in and out of my sight with an amazing coruscation.
The colour of this phenomenon was like burnished, or new washed silver. It shot with speed like
a star falling in the night. But it had a body much larger and a train longer than any
shooting star I have seen.*

Left:
*In Avebury Trusloe,
where two stones of the
ceremonial avenue of
stones from Avebury to
Beckhampton stand, this
star formation occurred
before evidence was
finally found for this
supposed second avenue.
(See* Prehistoric Sacred
Sites, vol. I *in this
series.)*

Vibrations

Many channellers and mediums, along with native people's prophecies, have claimed that the earth is undergoing a change in its vibrationary rate at this point in time. There is even evidence from NASA to suggest that the background radiation of the earth is rising. Most scientists agree that all matter is made of groups of particles vibrating on certain frequencies. Since we are made of matter, we, too, vibrate at certain frequencies, and are affected by other vibrations. The rising complexity of the crop circles are taken in by us unconsciously. Even the shapes of the simpler designs have an unconscious effect on us. Certain shapes are universally evocative by people across the globe and across time. Sometimes known as phenomes, shapes such as rings, spirals, circled rings and more strike a resonance in us for some unknown reason, perhaps because of a base vibration.

One thing is certain. Crop circles have the power to alter a person's life, at least in a spiritual sense. Almost everyone who has studied the phenomenon long enough has felt a change in the way they view the world and our place in it, whether they are serious researchers or hoaxers. There has been disillusionment, but there has also been a new understanding of the powers of unseen and untapped energies that are available – like all energy, for good or bad purposes.

As we delve ever more deeply into the world of computers, machines and cyberspace, a world where a few seconds can seem like an eternity, the earth (at least in some places) is crying out to us, showing that there is energy and power there, too, that has lain dormant for so long. Magical energy that is available for anyone who will take the time to listen to it and treat it with respect. Now, at the dawn of the 21st century, is the time to walk the path of our ancestors.

Alton Barnes Double Helix

Above:

17 June 1996. Alton Barnes, Wiltshire. Also known as the DNA *formation.*

Earth Energies

This design, first reported 17 June 1996, in the much-visited East Field, seems to represent the double helix of a strand of DNA. Nearly 650 feet long, and consisting of 89 circles, it also encompasses the spiritual energy of the area with its ends pointing to the ancient sites of Adam's Grave and Woodborough Hill.

This pictogram could have something to do with the theory that humankind need to raise their vibrations by making subtle changes in their DNA structure, in order to survive the coming new age. In addition, some studies have shown that the genetic structure in plants found inside crop circles is radically altered. It has also been shown that on some farms, at least, fields containing crop circles resulted in a higher yield than those without.

However, there is also the chance that this formation could be a fractal or resonance pattern.

There is beginning to be a greater acceptance of the theory that a giant grid of energy encloses the earth. This energy is unseen, but detectable by dowsing, with bent rods or pendulums.

Dowsing is an ancient art, and its results can vary from person to person. The dowser holds a pair of rods, made of branches, bent wire, crystal pendulums or even pieces of the crop itself, and walking slowly, waits for the rods to start turning, indicating that a field of energy has been crossed. Some say that a force acts upon the rods, others insist that the energy affects the dowser, causing minute muscular twitches that can be felt and interpreted. This energy runs everywhere throughout the earth. Some types of energy, however, run in more or less straight courses.

These energy lines, or leys, as they are known, can be most easily seen by looking at maps, and drawing a line through the tumuli, burial mounds, churches and other features of the landscape in a connect-the-dots fashion. Along these lines there are certain points, or nodes, of exceptional power or energy. These were revered by our ancestors, who built the great temples of Stonehenge, Avebury and Silbury on them, along with countless burial mounds and other tumuli. The leys seem to act as a magnet or beacon for UFOs, as many have been observed near ley lines. The same can be said for crop circles, which seem to form close to these bands of energy. One belief holds that crop circles are imprints of an energy beam as it strikes the earth, looking like a slice taken from the main beam, which is perceived by us as a formation on the ground.

Below:

East Field, Alton Barnes has seen many wonderful crop formations and this one, more than 1,000 feet long, is no exception. It appeared in barley in June 1999.

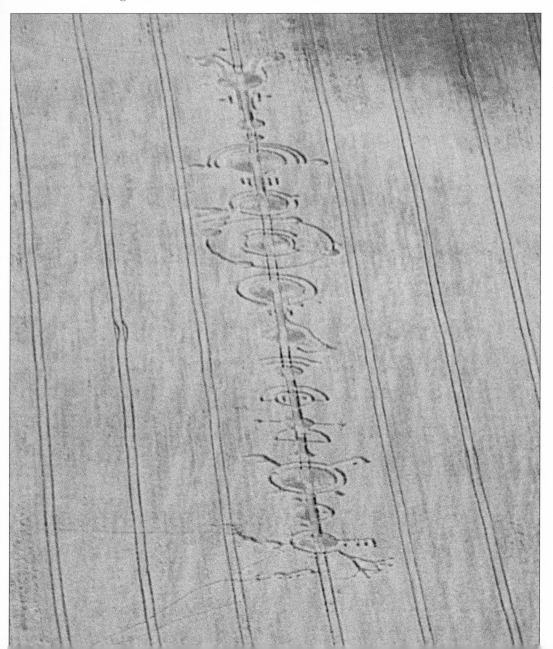

Some Notable Crop Formations

1970s and 1980s

15 August 1972. Starr Hill, Warminster, Wilts. Circles/triangles allegedly seen forming.
Summer 1975. Stonehenge, Wilts. Triangular triplet.
Summer 1978. Headbourne Worthy, Hants. First official quintuplet.
Summer 1978. Cheesefoot Head, Hants. Symmetrical triplet.
July 1981. Cheesefoot Head, Hants. Further symmetrical triplet, reported in media.
27 July 1984. Alfriston, E. Sussex. Quintuplet photographed by Denis Healey MP.
5 July 1986. Cheesefoot Head, Hants. Three ringed circles.
23 August 1986. Longwood Estate, Hants. First official Celtic Cross.
1 June 1987. Whiteparish, Wilts. Ringed circle w/pathway.
25 July 1987. Cheesefoot Head, Hants. Quintuplet, first official radial lay.
8 June 1988. Corhampton, Hants. Triangular triplet w/spoked lay.
July 1988. Silbury Hill, Wilts. Two quintuplets w/circles.
21 August 1989. Winterbourne Stoke, Wilts. Circle w/quartered lay.

1990

23 May. Chilcomb, Hants. First official pictogram. First 'boxes'.
6 June. Longwood Estate, Hants. Circle with broken rings.
16 June. Chilcomb, Hants. Triple-haloed dumb-bell.
June-July. Bishops Cannings, Wilts. Two Celtic Crosses, one superimposed.
11 July. Alton Barnes, Wilts. Much-publicised pictogram w/'claws'.
11 July. Stanton St Bernard, Wilts. Pictogram w/'claws'.
13 July. Crawley Down, Wilts. 'Boxed' pictogram.
25 July. Beckhampton, Wilts. 'Scrolls' & triangles.
26 July. East Kennett, Wilts. Pictogram w/ 'claws'.
4 August. Cheesefoot Head, Hants. Two pictograms, one large, one small.

1991

7 July. Alton Barnes, Wilts. Long pictogram.
10 July. Stonehenge, Wilts. 'Insectogram' & ringed circle.
17 July. Barbury Castle, Wilts. Complex triangular pictogram.
19 July. Alton Priors, Wilts. Slanted 'key' pictogram.
27 July. East Kennett, Wilts. Straight 'key' pictogram.
August. Milk Hill, Wilts. Hieroglyphic script.
1 August. Beckhampton, Wilts. Best of several 1991 'whales'.
12 August. Ickleton, Cambs. 'Mandelbrot Set' fractal.
15 August. Manton, Wilts. Clear video of light ball taken in pictogram.
18 August. Froxfield, Wilts. 'Serpent' or 'Brain'.

1992

9 July. Alton Barnes, Wilts. 'Snail' pictogram.
16 July. Milk Hill, Wilts. Circles & curved paths.
24 July. East Meon, Hants. Haloed pictogram.
24 July. Oliver's Castle, Wilts. Triangular triplet formed in response to meditation.
2 August. West Stowell, Wilts. Mercury astrological symbol.
9 August. Froxfield, Wilts. Long pictogram.
12 August. Alton Priors, Wilts. Ringed crescent.
16 August. Silbury Hill, Wilts. 'Charm Bracelet' ring.

1993

7 July. Charley Knoll, Loughborough, Leics. Complex cruciform pictogram.
11 July. East Kennett, Wilts. Ring encircling T-junction.
11 July. West Kennett, Wilts. 'Nautilus' & zigzag.
11 July. West Overton, Wilts. '666' emblem.
7 August. Cherhill, Wilts. 'Hands of Friendship' pictogram.
4 September. Bythorn, Cambs. 10-petalled mandala.

1994

7 July. Barbury Castle, Wilts. Crescents/circles 'insect'.
15 July. Bishops Cannings, Wilts. 'Scorpion'.

23 July. West Stowell, Wilts. 'Galaxy' star map. Best of three similar 1994 designs.

23-24 July. East Dean, W. Sussex. Two 'thought bubble' designs.

26 July. Ashbury, Oxon. Quarter-mile-long pictogram.

27 July. Oliver's Castle, Wilts. Nested crescents.

28 July. West Overton, Wilts. 'Infinity' symbol.

4 August. Froxfield, Wilts. 'Flower of Life'.

11/12 August. Avebury, Wilts. 'Web/dreamcatcher' emblem.

14 August. Avebury Trusloe, Wilts. 'Curled scorpion'.

1995

29 May. Beckhampton, Wilts. Spiral.

31 May. Alfriston, E. Sussex. 4-armed 'Catherine wheel'.

12 June. Telegraph Hill, Chilcomb, Hants. Quintuplet of quintuplets w/'aum' symbol.

20 June. Bishops Sutton, Hants. 'Asteroid belt'.

26 June. Longwood Estate, Hants. Solar system ('Earth missing') diagram.

29 June. Felbridge, W. Sussex. Rings & circles formed in response to meditation.

Mid-July. East Meon, Hants. Nested crescents.

6 July. Dunley, Hants. Multi-rings & 'intestine'.

7 July. Long Marston, Warwicks. 'Eye' emblem.

15 July. Cissbury Ring, W. Sussex. 'Time tunnel' rings.

23 July. Winterbourne Bassett, Wilts. Ringed squares.

1996

17 June. Alton Barnes, Wilts. 'DNA' double helix.

7 July. Stonehenge, Wilts. 'Julia Set' fractal, formed by day.

12 July. Littlebury Green, Essex. 6-petalled 'flower'.

26 July. Ashbury, Oxon. Vesica Pisces.

29 July. Etchilhampton, Wilts. 4100ft paths & circles.

29 July. Windmill Hill, Beckhampton, Wilts. Triple 'Julia Set' fractal.

Early August. Streatley, Barton-Le-Clay, Beds. Circles & semi-rings.

2 August. Liddington Castle, Wilts. 'Brooch' emblem & fractal.

11 August. Oliver's Castle, Wilts. 6-armed 'snowflake'. Claimed videoed forming.

1997

20 April. Barbury Castle, Wilts. 6-petalled flower.

4 May. Burderop Down, Wilts. Qabalah/'Tree of Life'.

1 June. Winterbourne Bassett, Wilts. 'Chinese puzzle'.

9 June. Stonehenge, Wilts. Hexagonal 'snowflake'.

11 July. Alton Barnes, Wilts. 'Torus knot'.

14 July. Cley Hill, Wilts. Spoked hexagon.

23 July. Silbury Hill, Wilts. 'Koch Snowflake' fractal.

1 August. Etchilhampton, Wilts. 6-armed star & 780-box grid.

8 August. Milk Hill, Wilts. 'Koch Snowflake' fractal.

18 August. Hackpen Hill, Wilts. 'Strange Attractor' fractal.

1998

3 May. West Kennett, Wilts. 'Beltane Wheel'.

19 June. Clanfield, Hants. Clustered rings & semi-circles.

20 June. Beckhampton, Wilts. 10 petals encircling pentagram.

4 July. Dadford, Bucks. Double pentagram w/'bird', ankh & 'Ganesha' symbols.

5 July. Danebury Ring, Hants. 7-petalled ring.

9 July. Alton Barnes, Wilts. 7-petalled mandala.

11 July. Lockeridge, Wilts. 'Dragon/bug'.

21 July. Beckhampton, Wilts. 'Manta Ray'.

7 August. Lockeridge, Wilts. 'Insect Queen'.

8 August. Beckhampton, Wilts. Double pentagram on pentagon.

9 August. Tawsmead Copse, West Stowell, Wilts. 7-sided mandala.

1999

2 May. Middle Wallop, Hants. Eclipse sequence.

23 May. Avebury Trusloe, Wilts. 'Biology' symbol.

31 May. Barbury Castle, Wilts. Hebrew Menorah.

12 June. Alton Barnes, Wilts. Multi-pictogram.

4 July. Hackpen Hill, Wilts. Triple-armed complex swirl.

16 July. Windmill Hill, Beckhampton, Wilts. Square of 288 circles.

18 July. Cherhill, Wilts. 9-pointed mandala.

19 July. Devil's Den, Wilts. Complex star on hexagon.

28 July. Beckhampton, Wilts. 3-D 'ribbon' emblem.

31 July. Roundway, Wilts. 14-armed star.

6 August. Bishops Cannings, Wilts. 7-armed 'basket weave' star.

The above list is of some circular highlights of the last thirty years selected by Andy Thomas (see the Bibliography). The circles are arranged chronologically. See Map on centre pages in conjunction with this.

Other Theories and Beliefs

Ancient symbols   Another idea is that many of the circles are ancient symbols that are peculiar to humans. Perhaps they have been dormant, unseen, until our time of need – like King Arthur. In fact, some Native Americans and other tribal groups have announced that because of the coming new millennium, and the great changes it will bring, mankind will be re-awakened to ancient symbols in order to raise our vibrations, even change our DNA. Crop circles and pictograms, as symbols, strike a resonance in us, as can be seen in the many circular mandalas, and even the cup and ring marks on ancient Celtic artwork. Circles are also highly revered by native groups, who view crop circles as medicine wheels.

The Earth itself   The Earth itself may be causing the circles. The Gaia theory holds that the earth is a living, breathing organism. The crop circles are the outward signs of where healing energy is being intelligently sent. The crop formations could also be a by-product of energy being given off as the earth tries to heal itself. They might also be likened to sore spots, or welts, that can occur on a diseased organism. In any case, they are an attempt by Gaia to warn us that our destructive, polluting ways cannot be tolerated much longer before something drastic has to be done.

The Military   The Military is often blamed for crop circles. Maybe they're killing two birds with one stone by testing a machine and looking for people's reactions to strange phenomena.

Extraterrestrials   Extraterrestrials provide another favourite theory. Perhaps beings from another planet or another time in our own future are trying to tell us something. That could be, and there have been

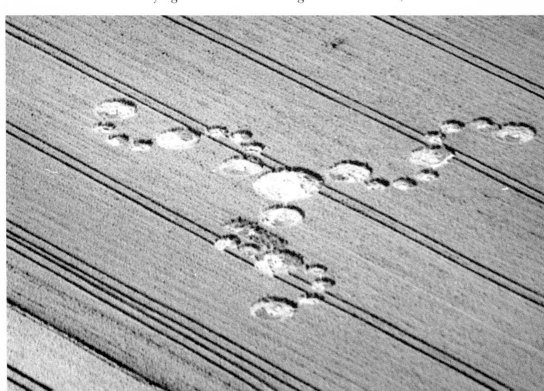

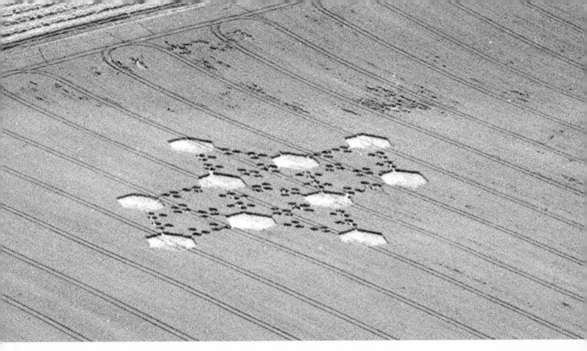

many cases of strange lights in the skies associated with crop circles. As a matter of fact, the modern circle phenomenon occurred just a few years after the famous Warminster UFO flap of the late 1970s, when you could hardly walk to the post box without seeing scores of interplanetary visitors hovering around. But if they were trying to communicate with us, why in the world would they choose to write unintelligible graffiti in corn crops in a remote part of southern England? Wouldn't they be better off holding a press conference at the White House? Or at the very least, you'd think they would make designs on a truly enormous scale, putting them down on the wheat fields of Kansas for instance, where extremely large fields are common.

The Wessex area, and Wiltshire in particular attracts crop circles partly because of its unique geological structure. The chalk downlands, lying on top of aquifers might act as a kind of geomagnetic battery, which holds and even magnifies certain types of energy. This, combined with the fact that very powerful energy lines like the St. Michael and St. Mary leys run through the area, could be the cause of the specific kind of energy needed. In fact, perhaps that's why our ancestors chose to build their amazing monuments like Stonehenge and Avebury here. Living in close proximity to the land, and literally dependent on it for their very lives, these Neolithic people could feel the power much more easily than we can.

Perhaps our ancestors knew how to create and unlock this energy themselves. Could they have made crop circles, maybe even using certain tones and rhythms to create cymatic patterns, to amplify energy? We don't know. Unless they made them in stone.

Above:
West Overton's huge matrix of hexagonal crystalline shape. Or is it an unfolded octagon? Some suggest that a 3D diamond with 8 sides can be formed by cutting around the edges and assembling into a 3D shape.

Ley Lines

Opposite:
This formation appeared in wheat near to the unexcavated East Kennet Longbarrow, in 1999.

Epilogue

In short, we still don't know who or what is making the crop circles. Our modern society, which bases 'truth' on science and empirical evidence, is always asking how? Could it be that to find the answer, we should be asking why? Why here in Wessex? – because of its soil and crops, or because of its long-standing tradition of mystery? Why now? – because the human race has the capacity to understand, or because we are on the cusp of a new era? Why crop circles – because they are non-threatening, or because they are tied to the fertility of the earth?

Regardless of who is making the circles, pictograms and symbols, they seem to strike a cord within us – a need for the excitement of something new, outside of our normal experience. They have already forced many people to re-think their view of the world. With the advances of science and technology (and the problems they bring), isn't it wonderful to still have a bit of magic and mystery in our lives?

What the future will bring to this field is anybody's guess. Each year we think 'Nothing can surpass this!' And with each new season, something does.

Glossary

Agriglyph - any pictorial or circular design formed in a field of crop.

Pictogram - any pictorial image, assumed to be a representation of another object.

Singleton - a single crop circle.

Lay - the swirled pattern on the floor of a crop circle. Usually counter- or clockwise.

Ley - an invisible, but detectable line of energy running close to the surface of the earth.

Aliens - intelligent beings not of this earth, usually thought of as coming from another planet.

Glyphs - any marking on the land that is more than a simple circle.

Whorls - plant stems that have been twisted together, like strands in a rope.

Swirl - the clockwise or counter-clockwise way in which a crop circle floor appears.

Cosmic - being of a universal, usually spiritual nature.

Cardioid - heart-shaped.

Arcane Symbols - symbols primarily used in magical, alchemical or esoteric teachings.

Julia Set - a mathematical object based on fractal design with continuously repeating design.

Mandlebrot - one of the most complex mathematical objects. Repeats in infinite variations.

Plasma Vortex - a column of highly charged ionised air that descends in a column or funnel. When the vortex touches the ground, the crop is spread outwards in a circular pattern.

Orgone - life energy, first investigated by psychoanalyst Wilhelm Reich in the 1940s.

Fractals - mathematical and geometrical objects that represent equations, especially in conjunction with the study of chaotic systems.

Chaos theory - a recent mathematical theory that studies and attempts to predict instability in natural systems.